Pupil Book 2

Karina Law

Focus on Literacy Pupil Book 2

Author: Karina Law

Series and cover design: Grasshopper Design Company

Design: Goodfellow and Egan, Cambridge

Editor: Mitzi Bales

Cover image: Kelvin Murray, Tony Stone Images

Illustrations: Tim Archbold, Stephanie Boey, Tayo Fatunla,
   Toni Goffe, Frances Jordan, Lorna Kent, Jan Lewis,
   Melanie Mansfield, Bethan Matthews, Andrew Midgley,
   Anette Isberg Rozijn, Mike Spoor, Martin Ursell,
   Amanda Welch

Published by Collins Educational
An imprint of HarperCollins*Publishers* Ltd
77–85 Fulham Palace Road
Hammersmith
London W6 8JB

Telephone ordering and information: 0870 0100 441

The HarperCollins website address is: www.**fire**and**water**.com

First published 1999
Reprinted 2000

Text © Karina Law 1999
Design and illustrations © HarperCollins*Publishers* Ltd 1999

Karina Law asserts the moral right to be identified
as the author of this work.

ISBN 0 00 302507 1

British Library Cataloguing in Publication Data
A catalogue record for this book is available from the
British Library.

Printed in Great Britain by Scotprint

www.Collins Education.com
On-line Support for Schools and Colleges

Acknowledgements
The author and publishers wish to thank the following for permission to use copyright material:
Unit 1: HarperCollins*Publishers* for extracts from *The Magical Bicycle* by Berlie Doherty, illustrated by Christian Birmingham (Picture Lions, 1996), text © Berlie Doherty, 1995; Unit 2: the author for "Street Sounds" from *Another Very First Poetry Book*, edited by John Foster (Oxford University Press, 1992), © 1992 by Jacqueline Brown; Unit 5: Penguin UK for extracts from *Granny's Quilt* by Penny Ives (Hamish Hamilton, 1993), text © Penny Ives, 1993; Unit 6: the author for extracts from *Tall Inside* (Methuen Children's Books, 1988), © Jean Richardson, 1988; Unit 7: HarperCollins*Publishers* for extracts from *Snowy* by Berlie Doherty, illustrated by Keith Bowen (1992), text © Berlie Doherty, 1992; Unit 8: Piccadilly Press for extracts from *A Worm's Eye View* by Jan Mark (1994), text © Jan Mark, 1994; Unit 9: Usborne Publishing, 83-85 Saffron Hill, London EC1N 8RT, for extract from *You and Your Child: Kitchen Fun* by Ray Gibson, © 1990 Usborne Publishing Ltd.; Unit 11: Kingfisher Books for extracts from "The Story of the Frog Princess" by Margaret Carter from *The Kingfisher Nursery Chest* (1991), text © Margaret Carter 1991; Unit 12: Walker Books Ltd for extracts and illustrations from *All Pigs are Beautiful* by Dick King-Smith (1993), text © 1993 by FoxBusters Ltd, illustrations © 1993 Anita Jeram; Unit 13: The Peters Fraser & Dunlop Group Ltd on behalf of the author, and Walker Books for extracts from "Dog, Cat and Monkey" from *South and North East and West*, edited by Michael Rosen (Walker Books, 1992), text © 1992 Michael Rosen, © 1992 OXFAM Activities; Unit 14: Sarah Matthews for "Chips" by Stanley Cook from *A Second Poetry Book*, edited by John Foster (Oxford University Press, 1980), © the estate of Stanley Cook; Unit 15: Karina Law for "What happens to the food we eat?"; Unit 16: Roy Yates Books for extracts from *The Raja's Big Ears*, told by Niru Desai (Jennie Ingham Associates, 1989), © Jennie Ingham Associates Ltd, 1989; Unit 18: Karina Law for "Why Do Snakes Shed their Skin?"; Unit 19: Zero to Ten Ltd for extracts and illustrations from *Lao Lao of Dragon Mountain* by Margaret Bateson-Hill (De Agostini Editions, 1996), © 1996 De Agostini Editions, text © 1996 Margaret Bateson-Hill, illustrations © 1996 Francesca Pelizzoli; Unit 20: Anderson Press Ltd, London, for extracts and illustrations © 1984, Susan Varley. First published by Anderson Press Ltd, London; Unit 22: Penguin UK for extracts and illustrations from *The Worst Witch* by Jill Murphy (Puffin, 1978), © Jill Murphy, 1974; Unit 23: A. P. Watt Ltd on behalf of Jill Murphy for "Author Bank" and extracts from "Questionnaire", produced by Book Trust's Children's Book Foundation (June 1993); Unit 24: A. P. Watt Ltd on behalf of the author for extracts from *The Hodgeheg* by Dick King-Smith (Hamish Hamilton Children's Books, 1987); Unit 25: Karina Law for "The Nation's Favourite Game"; Unit 26: The Watts Publishing Group for extracts from *Fangs* by Malorie Blackman (Orchard Books, 1998), text © Oneta Malorie Blackman; Unit 27: John Agard c/o Caroline Sheldon Literary Agency for "Hatch Me a Riddle" by John Agard from *Laughter Is An Egg* (Penguin Books, 1990); David Higham Associates for "Something I tell..." and "Hold it steady in your hand ..." by John Cunliffe from *Riddles and Rhymes and Rigmaroles* (Andre Deutsch, 1971); Unit 29: Karina Law for "How Do We Communicate?"; Unit 30: David Higham Associates on behalf of the estate of Roald Dahl, and Quentin Blake, for "Little Red Riding Hood and the Wolf" from *Revolting Rhymes* by Roald Dahl (Jonathan Cape, 1982).

Other sources
Unit 3: Egmont Children's Books for extracts from *The Pain and the Great One* by Judy Blume (William Heinemann, 1985), text © Judy Blume 1974, Trustee; Unit 4: Random House UK Ltd for extracts from *Sorry, Miss!* by Jo Furtado (Arrow/Beaver Books, 1989), text © 1987 by Jo Furtado; Unit 10: HarperCollins*Publishers* and the author for extracts from *Josie Smith at Christmas* by Magdalen Nabb (Young Lion, 1992); Unit 14: William Morrow & Co. for "Spaghetti! Spaghetti!" by Jack Prelutsky from *Rainy Rainy Saturday* (Greenwillow Books), © 1980 by Jack Prelutsky; Unit 17: David Higham Associates for extracts from "Why Snake Has No Legs" from *Creation Stories* (Walker Books, 1997), text © 1997 Ann Pilling; Unit 21: Penguin UK and A. P. Watt Ltd for extracts from "The Pudding Like a Night on the Sea" from *The Julian Stories* by Ann Cameron (Victor Gollancz, 1982); Unit 28: Gina Maccoby Literary Agency on behalf of the author for "Brother" by Mary Ann Hoberman, originally published in *Hello and Good-By* (Little, Brown & Co., 1959), © 1959, renewed 1987 by Mary Ann Hoberman.

Every effort has been made to trace copyright holders and to obtain their permission for the use of copyright material. The author and publishers will gladly receive any information enabling them to rectify any error or omission in subsequent editions.

Contents

Pupil Book 2

A New Bicycle

The Magical Bicycle

My best surprise
Was my shining bike
With its silver voice
But I couldn't ride it.

Every time I tried it
Threw me off.
I think it thought
It was a horse.

I bruised my knees.
I banged my chin.
I tried again, again, again.

Dad ran up the entry, holding on,
And then he ran all the way down
And panted all the way up again.

"Just turn your legs!"
He grew tired and slow,
"You won't fall off..."

And I never did
Till he let go.

from The Magical Bicycle *by Berlie Doherty, Collins*

The Magical Bicycle

A

1. What was the boy's best surprise?
2. What did the boy hurt when he fell off his bike?
3. Who was helping the boy learn to ride his bike?

B

1. The boy in the story is having trouble learning to ride his bicycle. What do you find difficult to do?
2. Do you think the boy will learn how to ride his bike in the end?

The long *i* sound

A Read the sentence below aloud (but quietly) and listen to the long **i** sound:

My best surpr**i**se was my b**i**ke but I couldn't r**i**de it.

1. Find three words in the sentence above with the long **i** sound. You will see that words with the long **i** sound often end with **e**.
2. Find five objects below that contain **i_e** and write their names.

B Write some sentences of your own using the **i_e** words below.

| like | slice | prize | inside |

1st prize

Your own experience

Write about something you have learned to do. It might be swimming, playing the recorder, tying your shoelaces or something else you remember well.

How long did it take you to learn?
Who helped you?
How did you feel when you finally did it?

Shoe Shuffle

Street Sounds

I love to hear my feet
as they're walking down the street
in wellies.
Blobble blabble blobble blabble
wobbly wellie feet.

I like to hear Jane's feet
when she's running down the street
in flip-flops.
Slit-slap, slit-slap
slittery slappery feet.

Listen to Mum's feet
parade along the street
in high heels.
Clock clop clock clop
swanky cloppy feet.

Hear my Grandma's feet
as she shuffles down the street
in slippers.
Shlur plock shlur plock
snorey slippery feet.

Jacqueline Brown

Different Shoes

A
1. Who runs down the street in flip-flops?
2. What sort of shoes is Mum wearing?
3. Who is wearing slippers?

B Which pair you would wear...
1. ...on the beach?
2. ...indoors?
3. ...for running?
4. ...in the rain?

trainers

wellies

flipflops

slippers

S, W

Days 2 and 3

Interesting sounds

A Jacqueline Brown has used words that begin with the same letters close together to make interesting sounds:

flip-**fl**ops   **cl**ock **cl**op

Copy these groups of words and choose a letter to put in each space.

1. _azy _ions
2. _ix _lithering _nakes
3. _ _eeky _ _ildren

B In her poem, Jacqueline Brown has described the **sounds** that different shoes make. Look at the pictures below and write a sentence to describe how they **look**.

1.

2.

3.

4.

5.

T

Days 4 and 5

Your new shoes

Write about a new pair of shoes.

Who took you to the shop?
Did you try the shoes on?

Describe the pair you got. How did you feel when you wore your new shoes for the first time?

The Pain and the Great One

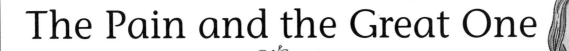

The Pain

My brother's a pain.
He won't get out of bed
In the morning.
Mum has to carry him
Into the kitchen.

He should get dressed himself.
But he's such a slowcoach
Daddy has to help him
Or he'd never be ready in time
And he'd miss the bus.

My brother the Pain
Is two years younger than me.
So how come
He gets to stay up
As late as I do?

When I got a phone call
He danced all around me
Singing stupid songs
At the top of his lungs.
Why does he have to act that way?

from The Pain and the Great One *by Judy Blume*

The Pain

A
1. Who carries the Pain into the kitchen for breakfast?
2. Who helps him to get dressed?
3. What does the Pain do when there is a phone call?

B
1. Who is telling this story?
2. What do you think is most annoying about the Pain?

Words and sentences

My brother is a pain.

A Copy the sentences below and choose the correct **ai** word to write in each space.

1. I saw the film _____ because it was so funny.

   afraid/again

2. I stayed home because I had a _____ in my tummy.

   pain/grain

3. The squirrel had a bushy _____.

   trail/tail

4. I asked my teacher to _____ the question.

   explain/complain

B Write about your brother or sister. What do you like best about them? What don't you like about them? If you haven't got one, write about the sort of brother or sister you would like.

Instructions

Write a set of instructions for the Pain on "How to annoy your big sister".
Use ideas from the story.

Sorry Miss

Sorry, Miss Folio...

We went to the circus last Saturday
and I took your book to read
while I was waiting...

but I waved it at my friend and this
huge elephant snatched it off me...

but my dad got it back only he'd sat
on it by then...

and my mum is still trying to
flatten it out for you...

Sorry, Miss Folio...

I was reading your book to
the gnome in our garden
because it's a good story...

and my mum called me in
for tea and the gnome said
he wanted to finish the
book so I left it for him...

only it rained and the
book got a bit wet...

and my mum's still drying
it out for you...

from Sorry Miss *by Jo Furtado*

Telling the truth

A

1. Where did the little boy say he took his book last Saturday?
2. How did the book get squashed?
3. Who was the boy reading his book to in the garden?
4. Why did the book get wet?

B

1. Do you think the little boy is telling the truth?
2. What do you think Miss Folio will have to say about all the excuses?

The short *oo* sound

Listen to the short **oo** sound in the sentence below.

I was reading your b**oo**k to the gnome in our garden because it's a g**oo**d story.

A Choose the correct word from the box to complete the sentences below.

hood	stood	cook	wool

1. My mum is a terrible _____ because she burns everything.
2. My coat has a _____ on it which keeps my head warm.
3. I _____ in the rain for an hour, waiting for a bus.
4. My jumper is made of _____.

B The letter **u** in the following words has the same sound as **oo** in b**oo**k.

pull	push	put

Choose the correct word from above to complete the following sentences.

1. We had to _____ the car because it would not start.
2. The teacher _____ my painting on the wall.
3. I did not want to _____ my wobbly tooth out.

Making excuses

Think of a good excuse to tell your teacher about why you didn't do your homework.

Think of something no one else has said before.

Granny's Quilt

I have the best granny in the world. I love going to stay with her and her two cats Fred and Mr Big, and I always ask Granny to tell me the story of her wonderful patchwork quilt. And Granny always says: "Do you really want to hear that old nonsense again? I must have told you about the quilt a thousand times. You know, it's like the story of my life. The little pieces are from all my different dresses, ever since I was a small girl just like you."

"I had ten brothers and sisters. My mother, who was a dressmaker, made all our clothes. Mine were usually hand-me-downs, but I had a new dress of my very own for my baby sister Emily's christening. It was made from this lovely blue spotty material."

"These squares are from my school pinafore. I hated the dark blue cloth! I was always being told off in school for day dreaming."

from Granny's Quilt *by Penny Ives*

Granny's memories

A

1. How many brothers and sisters did Granny have?
2. What colour was Granny's school pinafore?
3. Why was Granny always being told off in school?
4. Draw your favourite thing to wear. What material is it made from?

B

1. What are "hand-me-downs"?
2. When did Granny have a dress of her very own?
3. What material was her very own dress made from?

Clothing

A Choose the correct label to go with each of the pictures below.

jeans	jumper	skirt	socks
	shirt	trousers	

B

1. Make a list of the clothes you are wearing today.
2. Write about the colours and the materials of your clothes.

1.

2.

3.

4.

5.

6.

Party clothes

Write about a special party or celebration that you remember.

What did you wear?

How did you look and feel?

Tall Inside

Joanne was small for her age. She was the shortest person in her class.

"You'll catch up one of these days," her mother said, as if it didn't matter.

"All the best things come in small packages," her father said, giving her a kiss.

"You could try eating rubber bands. Then you might stretch," her brother Matt said.

They just didn't understand.

Most days Jo went next door to play with her best friend Jenny. They had just learned how to do handstands.

One day Jenny's cousins Rosie and Ann joined them. "Let's start a club," said Rosie, who couldn't do handstands. "To join you have to pass a test. Everyone has to jump up and swing from that branch."

Rosie did it easily, because she was tall. Jenny and Ann just made it. Jo couldn't reach at all.

"You can't join," Rosie told her. "You're too short."

"I don't want to join your silly club anyway," said Jo. And ran off home.

But she did.

from Tall Inside *by Jean Richardson*

Jo's sadness

A
1. What was different about Jo?
2. What did Matt tell Jo to try?
3. Who was Jo's best friend?

B How did Jo feel when Rosie said she could not join the club?

Making things right

A Read the names in the box below, which are from the story, *Tall Inside*.

What is wrong?

When you have spotted the mistake, write the names out correctly.

> 1. joanne   2. matt   3. jenny
> 4. rosie   5. ann

B Read these sentences aloud and listen to the **oy** sound in each.

> Jo and Jenny enj**oy**ed doing handstands.
> Jo wanted to j**oi**n the club.

Copy the sentences below and write **oy** or **oi** in each space. Check your spelling in a dictionary.

1. My little brother can be very ann_ _ing.
2. He is always trying to sp_ _l my games.
3. My little brother often breaks my t_ _s.
4. He makes too much n_ _se when I am watching television.

Your feelings

Have you ever felt sad because a friend was unkind to you?

Write about what happened and how it made you feel. Are you friends again now?

Snowy

Rachel doesn't live in a house.

She lives in a kind of barge called a narrowboat, on a kind of river called a canal. Her boat is painted yellow and red and blue. There are castles and roses painted on the side of it, and buckets and kettles on the roof.

At night, when she goes to bed, she can feel the narrowboat rocking gently from side to side. She can hear the slish! slosh! of water against its sides. She loves her narrowboat.

It's called Betelgeuse, which is a kind of star, but Rachel calls it Beetle Juice. The best thing about living on a boat, better than the rocking at night, better than the castles and roses, better than the splish! splash! of the water on its sides, is Snowy.

Snowy is the boat horse. She lives in a stable on the banks of the canal, and her job is to pull Beetle Juice along the water.

When Mum clicks her tongue and says, "Come on, Snowy," she lowers her head and pulls. Then she plod, plod, plods along the towpath, and her long rope stretches behind her, and Beetle Juice floats along the canal path like a painted swan.

from **Snowy** *by* **Berlie Doherty, Collins**

16

Rachel's home

A
1. Where does Rachel live?
2. What does Rachel like best about where she lives?
3. What does she call her home?

B
1. What are painted on the side of Rachel's home?
2. Where does Snowy live?
3. What would you like best about living in a boat?

S, W

Days 2 and 3

Some *ar* words

Rachel lives in kind of a b**ar**ge.

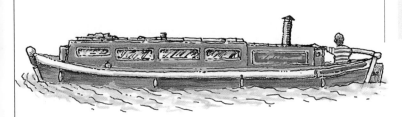

A Choose the correct **ar** word to complete each sentence below.

arm	bark	farm	garden
party	sharks		

1. We heard the dog _ _ _ _ at the stranger.
2. I hope there are no _ _ _ _ _ _ swimming in the sea.
3. We have not got a _ _ _ _ _ _ because we live in a block of flats.
4. Old Mac Donald had a _ _ _ _.

B Label each of the pictures below. Use the words in the box.

barge	lighthouse	castle	treehouse

1.

2.

3.

4.

Different sorts of homes

Think of a different sort of place where you would like to live.

Write about what it would be like to live there.

A Worm's Eye View

The allotments were behind the house, at the end of the garden.

When they reached the iron gates, Mum let David get out of the buggy.

"You can walk on the nice grass," said Mum. David growled and stamped on the nice grass. Every time he saw a daisy he squashed it.

They parked the buggy and Dad told them what to do.

"I am going to hoe the onions," he said. "Alice can weed round the cabbages and Tom can pull up carrots."

"ME," said David.

Alice took the trowel out of the pram and gave it to David. He found some more daisies and hit them on the head.

"Dead. Dead," David said.

"Keep an eye on him," Mum said. "Don't let him wander off."

After a bit David started to dig.

"Plant," David said. "Now."

Tom picked up a twig. "Plant that," he said. "It might grow into a tree." David put the twig in the hole and banged down the earth all around it.

"More plant," David said.

from A Worm's Eye View *by Jan Mark*

Looking after David

A

1. What did David do to the daisies?
2. What was Tom's job?
3. What tool did David use to dig?
4. Do you think Tom and Alice liked looking after David?

B

1. What is an allotment?
2. What did Tom say the twig might grow into?
3. How would you describe David?

The *ou* sound

Listen **ou**t for the **ow** sound!

A Write out the sentences below and underline **ow** and **ou**.

1. The allotments were behind the house.
2. David growled and stamped on the nice grass.
3. Alice took the trowel and gave it to David.
4. David found some daisies and hit them on the head.

B Copy the labels below. Write **ow** or **ou** in each space. Check your spelling in a dictionary.

1. m_ _se

2. cl_ _n

3. fl_ _er

4. h_ _se

5. _ _l

6. m_ _th

Your own story

Imagine what would happen if Alice and Tom took David to the supermarket. Write a story about some of the things David might do.

Home Grown

Cress Creatures – Woolly Sheep

You will need: cress seeds, a jug of cold water, a dinner plate, brown or black felt or paper, scissors, a scrap of white felt or paper, cotton wool, a black felt-tip pen.

1. Pull some cotton wool into a rough shape for the sheep's body and lay it on a plate.

2. Cut out some ears, a face and some legs in black felt and lay them on the cotton wool.

3. Cut the eyes out of white felt and mark in the centre with a black felt-tip pen.

4. Add some extra cotton wool for the forehead and tail.

5. Wet the cotton wool.

6. Sprinkle some cress seeds over the cotton wool.

7. Keep the cotton wool and cress moist by pouring a little water onto the plate each day.

*From **Kitchen Fun** by Ray Gibson*

20

Making a cress creature

A
1. What is used to make the body of the sheep?
2. What are the sheep's legs made from?
3. How many instructions must you follow?

B
1. Why do you need to keep the cotton wool moist?
2. Do you think it would matter if the instructions were in a different order?

Correct order

A These instructions have been jumbled up. Write them out in the correct order.

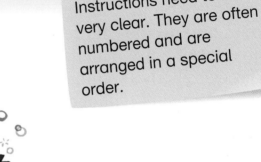

Instructions need to be very clear. They are often numbered and are arranged in a special order.

1. Finally, dry your hair with a towel.

2. Then rub shampoo into your hair.

3. First of all, rinse your hair to make it wet.

4. Rinse away the shampoo.

B Read the following bedtime tasks.

Write them out in the order that you do them and number them.

Clean my teeth.

Get undressed.

Put on my bedclothes.

Say goodnight.

Have a bath.

Close my curtains.

Remember, your list will probably be in a different order from your friend's.

Writing instructions

Write instructions for cleaning out a hamster cage. Remember to number your instructions.

Josie Smith at Christmas

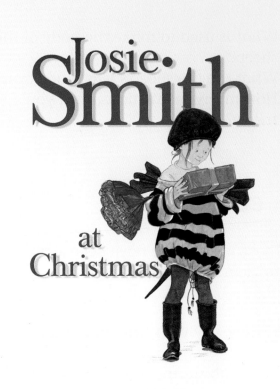

It was a dark and snowy afternoon. The lights were on in Josie Smith's classroom and all the children were making a lot of noise. The floor was wet from everybody's wellingtons, there was a smell of school dinner, and wet gloves were drying on the radiators because they'd all been snowballing and sliding and falling in the yard.

"Quiet, everybody," Miss Valentine said. But they were all shouting and pushing and nobody could hear.

"If you've all got your gym shoes on," Miss Valentine said, "start moving your tables and chairs. And do it quietly!"

They started moving their tables and chairs but they didn't do it quietly. They pushed and shoved and crashed and banged and shouted and argued and scraped and bumped, and then the door opened and Miss Potts, the headmistress, marched in.

"How dare you!" shouted Miss Potts, "How dare you make all this noise that I can hear from my office!"

Everybody stopped. It went so quiet that you could hear the children breathing, and Josie Smith could hear her own chest going bam bam bam because she was frightened of Miss Potts.

*from **Josie Smith at Christmas** by Magdalen Nabb, Collins*

The story

A

1. Who is Miss Potts?
2. Why did Miss Potts march into Josie's classroom?
3. What happened when Josie was frightened?

B

1. At what time of year was this story set?
2. What was the weather like?
3. What do you think will happen next?

S, W

Days 2 and 3

Past tense

Read how Josie's class moved the tables and chairs:

They **pushed** and **shoved** and **crashed** and **banged** and **shouted** and **argued** and **scraped** and **bumped**.

> The action words in this sentence end with **ed** because the actions happened in the past.

Give me those or I'll push you in the puddle.

The bully pushed me into a puddle.

Read the two sentences above. Explain why **push** changes to **pushed** in the second sentence.

A Write out the sentences and change the words in **bold** so that they make sense.

1. Mum **shout** at me because I left my bedroom in a mess.
2. Last week I **score** an amazing goal during football practice.
3. I **ask** my teacher to explain the sum again.

4. I **scrape** my knee when I fell off my bike.

B Write some sentences of your own using the words below.

| looked | worked | landed | called |

T

Days 4 and 5

Writing

Write a short story of your own about Josie Smith's class.

Imagine that somebody has broken a window during playtime.

What will Miss Potts say about it?

A Kiss from a Princess

Once upon a time there lived a princess whose favourite toy was a golden ball. Every day she would go into the gardens of her father's palace and play with her golden ball.

Then one day as the princess stretched out her hands to catch the ball it slipped through her fingers. Across the grass it bounced and PLOP! into the waters of the deep, deep well it went.

How the princess cried! Tears ran down her cheeks until, through her sobs, she heard a small voice say, "Don't cry, Princess. If I get you back your ball what will you give me in return?"

And there, looking at her with his big sad eyes, was a very large frog. "Oh anything, anything!" cried the princess.

"All I want," said the frog, "is to be your companion. I should like to play with you, to eat with you at your table and at night to sleep in your bed."

"Oh I promise, I promise," cried the princess and, straight away, the frog dived into the waters of the deep, deep well and, moments later, returned with the golden ball.

But the princess – who secretly thought frogs were nasty, slimy creatures – snatched the ball and ran back as fast as she could to the palace, leaving the poor frog all on his own.

From **The Story of the Frog Prince**
retold by Margaret Carter

The Frog Prince

A
1. What was the princess's favourite toy?
2. Why was the princess crying?
3. What did the frog want?

B
1. What did the princess think about frogs?
2. Did the princess keep her promise?
3. What do you think will happen next?

S, W

Days 2 and 3

The *ph* sound

Listen to the sound **f** at the beginning of **f**rog.

The same sound can also be heard in words with **ph**.

When **p** is followed by **h** the sound is **f** for **f**rog, not **p** for **p**rincess.

A Look at the pictures below. Write the correct word for each and underline the **ph** sounds.

photograph   dolphin   elephant
phone   trophy

1.

2.

3.

4.

5.

B Write two or three sentences using any of the above words.

T

Days 4 and 5

Continuing the story

Continue the story of *The Frog Prince*.

Write what happens next.

Will there be a happy ending?

All Pigs are Beautiful

I love pigs. I don't care if they're little pigs or big pigs, with long snouts or short snouts, with ears that stick up ears or that flop down. I don't mind if they're black or white or ginger or spotty. I just love pigs.

Though of all the pigs I ever owned, my one particular favourite was a boar called Monty, who was a Large White.

Monty never looked very white, because he lived out in a wood where there was a pond in which he liked to wallow.

Sows spend their lives having babies, and they take as good care of them as

A good coating of mud protects a pig from sunburn.

your mum does of you. Well, almost. Trouble is, newborn piglets are so small that sometimes the sow lies down and squashes one. Your mother would never do that to you – I hope!

A sow normally has between eight and twelve piglets at a time.

From All Pigs are Beautiful
by Dick King-Smith

Information about pigs

A

1. What was Dick King-Smith's favourite pig called?
2. What are newborn pigs called?
3. What does mud protect a pig from?

B

1. Is this **fiction** or **non-fiction**?
2. What do you like most about pigs?

Opposites

Dick King-Smith likes **little** pigs or **big** pigs, with **long** snouts or **short** snouts.

little is the opposite of **big**	**long** is the opposite of **short**

A Read the words in **bold**. Think of an opposite word to describe each picture.

1. A **small** fish

   A _____ whale

2. A **cold** drink

   A _____ bath

3. A **wet** dog

   A _____ towel

4. A **hard** rock   A _____ pillow.

B There has been a robbery! Write out the sentences below. Choose the words that you think describe the picture best.

1. It was **dark/light**.
2. The robber was **tall/short**.
3. The robber's sack was **full/empty**.

Glossaries

Many information books have a **glossary**. A glossary tells you the meaning of some of the words. It is a bit like a dictionary.

Make up a glossary to explain the words below.

Explain each word in one or two sentences.

Use information books and dictionaries to help you.

boar **piglet** **snout** **sow** **trotter**

Dog, Cat and Monkey

A Folk Tale from Indonesia

Dog and Cat are fighting over some meat. Dog's got his jaws round the bone, Cat's got his claws into the flesh. They heave and they tug, but the moment Dog thinks he's got it, Cat gives it a tug. Then the moment Cat thinks he's got it, Dog gets his teeth round a bit more. Neither of them is winning.

Monkey comes to have a look. Soon he's dancing around giving advice: "Go on, Cat, go for it with the claws, now the teeth. You've got him now, Dog. Grind those jaws. Don't growl, it'll weaken your grip. Give it a shake, Cat, it'll throw him. Hang on in there, Dog..." and so on.

Dog and Cat start getting tired. Cat has an idea.

While he's hanging on with his claws, he shouts to Monkey, "Say

Monkey, any chance you could help us here? Couldn't you share it out between us so we each had equal parts?"

Monkey calls back, "I'd love to. We'll just set up some scales to make sure everything's fair, right?"

from **The Oxfam Book of Children's Stories**
edited by Michael Rosen

28

Dog and Cat

A
1. What are Dog and Cat fighting about?
2. Who do they ask to help them?
3. What do you think will happen in the end?

B
1. What do you think the scales will be used for?
2. How would you sort out this fight if Cat and Dog asked for your help?

Different tenses

The story *Dog, Cat and Monkey* is written as if it is happening now.

A
1. Read the two sentences below and see if you can spot the changes. Write down the words that have changed.

   a) Cat and Dog both want the meat. Monkey sees them fighting. He gives them advice.

   b) Cat and Dog both wanted the meat. Monkey saw them fighting. He gave them advice.

2. Which sentence is written as if it is happening now (in the **present**)?
3. Which sentence is written as if it has already happened (in the **past**)?

B Write out the sentences below. Write the word that makes sense in each space.

1. Last night my mum _____ me to phone my gran.

   tell/told

2. I _____ a whale swimming in the sea last year.

   saw/see

3. My cat _____ a bird in the garden yesterday.

   catch/caught

4. Last summer we _____ to the beach.

   go/went

Monkey's story

Pretend you are Monkey.

Write about the fight that you saw between Dog and Cat.

Write your story as if it has already happened (in the **past**).

How did you sort it out?
Who got the meat in the end?

Food From Far and Wide

Chips

Out of the paper bag
Comes the hot breath of the chips
And I shall blow on them
To stop them burning my lips.

Before I leave the counter
The woman shakes
Raindrops of vinegar on them
And salty snowflakes.

Outside the frosty pavements
Are slippery as a slide
But the chips and I
Are warm inside.

Stanley Cook

Spaghetti! Spaghetti!

Spaghetti! spaghetti!
you're wonderful stuff,
I love you, spaghetti,
I can't get enough.
You're covered with sauce
and you're sprinkled with cheese,
spaghetti! spaghetti!
oh, give me some please.

Spaghetti! spaghetti!
piled high in a mound,
you wiggle, you wriggle,
you squiggle around.
There's slurpy spaghetti
all over my plate,
spaghetti! spaghetti!
I think you are great.

from **Spaghetti! Spaghetti!,**
Jack Prelutsky

The poems

A Read *Chips* by Stanley Cook

1. What are the chips in?
2. How does the poet cool the chips down?
3. Can you find two words that begin with **sl** and are close together?
4. Which line do you like best in this poem?

B Read *Spaghetti! Spaghetti!* by Jack Prelutsky

1. Which word in the first verse rhymes with **cheese**?
2. Which word in the second verse rhymes with **plate**?
3. What is the same in the words **wiggle**, **wriggle** and **squiggle**?
4. Which of the two poems on this page do you like best?

Commas in lists

I like to eat slugs, spiders, flies and worms.

When we write a list of more than two things, we need to use commas.

A

1. How many commas are there in the sentence above?
2. Write a list of four things you like to eat. Begin your sentence like this:
   I like to eat...
3. Write a list of four things you don't like to eat. Begin your sentence like this:
   I don't like to eat ...

B Write out the sentences below. Put in the missing commas.

1. People in Italy like to eat pasta pizza spaghetti and ice-cream.
2. Apples oranges bananas and pears are different kinds of fruit.
3. Carrots cabbages potatoes and peas are all vegetables.

Your poem

Write a poem about your favourite food. Describe the taste of it.

What is it that you love about it?

Begin your poem like this:

I love _____
I can't get enough ...

The Food We Eat

What Happens to the Food We Eat?

People need food to keep their bodies working in the same way that a car needs petrol.

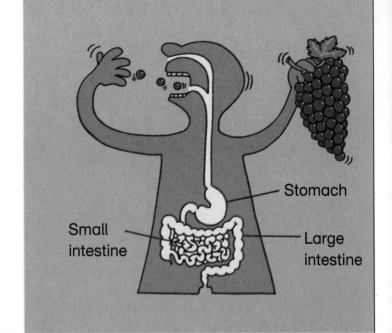

Stomach

Small intestine

Large intestine

When you feel hungry your body is telling you that it needs food.

When you swallow food it travels down a tube into your stomach.

From your stomach, the food you eat travels down long tubes called intestines.

Special chemicals break the food up into tiny pieces.

From here the waste food then passes out of your body when you use the toilet.

It usually takes about a day and a night for your body to digest a meal.

Information about food

A

1. How do you know when your body needs food?
2. Where does the food that you eat travel to first?
3. How long does it take to digest a meal?

B

1. What are your **intestines**?
2. What happens to the waste food?

S, W

Days 2 and 3

Using an index

An **index** helps you to find the information you are looking for. It tells you which page to turn to.

The **index** is usually at the back of an information book.

This is the **index** from a book about eating. An index is in alphabetical order.

A

1. Which page would you look on to find out about taste buds?
2. Which page would you turn to if you wanted to learn about teeth?
3. What information is on page 25?

Index

diet 26, 27	stomach 12, 13
digestion 4,5	swallowing 11
energy 22, 24	taste buds 9
exercise 24	teeth 10
food 25	tongue 9
germs 12	vitamins 22
intestines 18, 19	waste 18
mouth 9	water 18

B Find an information book with an index.

Work with a partner. Take it in turns to look up something interesting, using the index.

A class dictionary

Choose six or more of your favourite foods. List them in alphabetical order.

Draw pictures and write descriptions.

Make a class dictionary of food.

The Raja's Big Ears

Once upon a time there was a Raja who had big ears. He always wore a topee to cover them, as he thought his subjects would laugh at him if they saw them.

The people did not know why the Raja wore a topee. But they admired their King, so they decided to copy him. Soon everyone was wearing a topee.

Now, the Raja had a Royal Barber called Manji, who of course, knew the secret of the Raja's big ears. But the Raja had warned him never to say a word to anyone.

Manji was just bursting to tell someone, but he was afraid of what the Raja might do to him if he did tell. He might have Manji's ears chopped off!

One day Manji went for a walk in the jungle to think in peace and quiet. Suddenly he had the answer – he would tell his secret to a tree!

So he found a wide, tall tree. He sat down on the ground, looked up into the branches, and said: "Oh tree, I must tell you this. If I don't tell someone I shall burst … *Our Raja has big ears!* And to hide them he wears a topee – all the time!"

The leaves on the tree rustled in the breeze.

from **The Raja's Big Ears** *retold by Niru Desai*

Day 1 The Raja's secret

A
1. Why did the Raja wear a topee?
2. Who knew about the Raja's secret?
3. What did the barber think the Raja might do if he told anyone the secret?

B
1. What does a barber do?
2. Why did the Raja's people wear a topee?
3. Why did Manji think it would be safe to tell the secret to a tree?
4. What do you think people would say if they found out about the Raja's big ears?

S, W

Days 2 and 3 The *ear* sound (as in bear)

Listen to the sound **ear** in the word **ear**s.

In other words the sound is different. Listen to the sound **ear** in the word b**ears**.

The same sound can be written in other ways:

| bear | chair | hare |

A Write out the sentences below. Choose the correct word to write in each space.

| scared | pear | square | hair | pair |

1. A _____ has four sides and four corners.
2. A _____ is a tasty, green fruit.
3. Yesterday I got a new _____ of shoes.
4. I felt _____ on the ghost train ride.
5. I have straight _____ but my sister's is curly.

B Write some sentences of your own using the words below.

| stare | care | wear | air |

 T

Days 4 and 5 Descriptions

Describe the two main characters in this story, the Raja and Manji.

Write all that you know about them.

Write something that the Raja and Manji might say.

Why Snake Has No Legs

A Story from Ghana

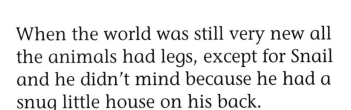

When the world was still very new all the animals had legs, except for Snail and he didn't mind because he had a snug little house on his back.

One day they decided to build a new farm and plant extra crops. This was hard work, so they agreed to do it together. But on the first day Snake, who was a bit of an idle fellow, said his great aunt was coming to see him and he would have to stay at home. The other animals went off to begin cutting the trees down and by nightfall they'd made a good start.

It was no thanks to Snake, though; he really was lazy. Next morning he said he had a bad cold. Every morning brought a new excuse. The animals grew tired of him.

All the animals worked hard and at last a wonderful harvest was ready to gather in. All their hard work had been worthwhile. But the night before they were to reap the first crop a terrible thing happened. Someone stole it. And this happened again and again, night after night. The poor animals were heart-broken and they sent for the spider, Ananse, because, of all creatures, he was by far the cleverest. He listened very carefully.

Then he said, "Don't worry, I have a plan."

from **Why Snake Has No Legs** *retold by Ann Pilling*

Snake's story

A

1. What excuse did Snake give on the second day?
2. Who was the cleverest creature of all?

B

1. What do you think Ananse is planning?
2. Think of a plan to catch the thief and write it down.

S, W

Days 2 and 3

The *wh* sound

A Answer the following questions about the story.

1. Why were the animals tired of Snake?
2. Who do you think was stealing the crops?
3. When were the crops taken?
4. What is the name of the animal with a house on its back?

Look at the words at the beginning of each question above. What two letters begin each of the words?

B Write down the names of the pictures below. The words all begin with **wh**.

1.

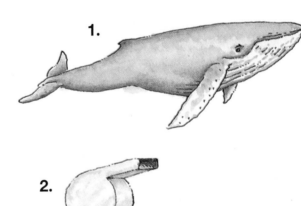

2.

3.

4.

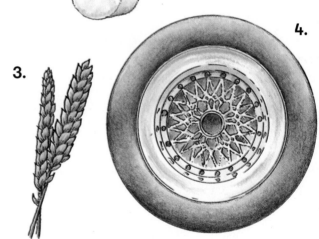

T

Days 4 and 5

Your animal story

Write a story of your own about an animal. You might explain why the robin has a red front, why the penguin cannot fly or why the giraffe has a long neck. Or you may like to think up an idea of your own. Begin your story like this:

When the world was still very new …

Snake Charm

Why Do Snakes Shed Their Skin?

As a snake grows, its skin becomes very tight and the snake needs to shed it. This usually takes a few days. When a snake is about to shed its skin, its eyes turn milky white. The snake is nearly blind at this stage so it hides away from danger.

When the snake is ready, it rubs its mouth on a hard object, such as a rock, to peel away the first bit of skin. Then it wriggles its way out of the old skin turning it inside out like a sock. Underneath is a new, bright and shiny body. The snake will continue to grow and soon it will need to shed its skin again.

The snake's skin

A

1. How long does it take a snake to shed its skin?
2. What happens to the snake's eyes?

B

1. Why does the snake hide when it is ready to shed its skin?
2. How does the snake begin to shed its skin?

S, W

Days 2 and 3

More about the index

This is the **index** from a book about snakes.

Index

boa 13
cobra 14
eyes 10
fangs 14
feeding 7, 8
viper 15
moving 4
nests 16
poisonous snakes 14, 15
python 12
rattlesnake 15
scales 9
shedding skin 10

A

1. Which pages would you look on to find out about poisonous snakes?
2. Which pages would you turn to if you wanted to find out what snakes eat?
3. What information is on page 16?

B

1. Indexes are in alphabetical order. Which word in the index opposite is in the wrong place?
2. Find an information book with an index. Work with a partner.

Take it in turns to use the index and look up something interesting.

T

Days 4 and 5

An explanation

How does a snake shed its skin?
Write a step-by-step explanation.

Lao Lao of Dragon Mountain

Long ago in the country of China there lived an old woman. She was known to everyone as Lao Lao and she lived in a tiny village in the foothills of the mountain where the Ice Dragon reigned.

Her greatest pleasure was to sit outside her home surrounded by the children of the village. There she would take a thin sheet of paper and the small pair of scissors that she kept in her front pocket, and while she cut she sang,

Fold it and cut it and turn it around
Open it up and see what you've found.

So beautiful were these paper-cuts that the fame of the old woman spread. People from the towns started to climb up the steep, narrow path to ask Lao Lao for one of her paper-cuts.

They would always find her sitting outside her house, busy with her scissors and singing,

Fold it and cut it and turn it around
Open it up and see what you've found.

And the children would watch in amazement as she unfolded the piece of paper – what would it be?
A butterfly! A cockerel! A flower!
Lao Lao would watch the children running home, each holding their own special gift. And as they ran, she would hear them singing,

Fold it and cut it and turn it around
Open it up and see what you've found.

from **Lao Lao of Dragon Mountain**
by Margaret Bateson-Hill

Lao Lao's life

A
1. Which country does Lao Lao live in?
2. What sort of creature reigned in Lao Lao's village?
3. What did Lao Lao do with paper and scissors?

B
1. What creatures could Lao Lao make from paper?
2. If you met Lao Lao, what would you ask her to make for you?

The *er* sound

Read the sentence below and listen to the **er** sound.

> Lao Lao sat outside h**er** home and made pap**er** butt**er**flies and flow**er**s.

The same sound can sometimes be heard in words with **ir** and **ur**.

A Write the correct label to go with each picture and underline the **er**, **ir** and **ur** sounds.

> bird   church   spider   girl
> computer   nurse

B Write two or three sentences of your own, using any of the words below.

> first   over   hurt   turn
> thirsty   later

1.

2.

3.

5.

4.

6.

Lao Lao's village

Think about the place where Lao Lao lives. Write about this place using information from the story.

Think of words to describe the village.

Write about the Ice Dragon. Do you think it is friendly or frightening?

Badger's Parting Gifts

Badger had always been there when anyone needed him. The animals all wondered what they would do now that he was gone. Badger had told them not to be unhappy, but it was hard not to be. As spring drew near, the animals often visited each other and talked about the days when Badger was alive.

Badger had shown Mrs Rabbit how to bake gingerbread rabbits.

 Mole was good at using scissors, and he told about the time Badger had taught him how to cut out a chain of moles from a piece of folded paper.

Frog was an excellent skater. He recalled how Badger had helped him take his first slippery steps on the ice.

Each of the animals had a special memory of Badger – something he had taught them that they could now do extremely well. He had given them each a parting gift to treasure always.

Fox remembered how, when he was a young cub, he could never knot his tie properly until Badger showed him how.
Fox could now tie every knot ever invented and some he'd made up himself.

from **Badger's Parting Gifts**
by Susan Varley, Collins

Badger and his friends

A
1. What did Badger teach Mole?
2. Which animal did Badger teach how to skate?
3. What did Badger teach Fox to do?
4. What did Mrs Rabbit learn from Badger?

B
1. Why were the animals sad?
2. If you had been a friend of Badger, what would you have liked him to teach you?

More opposites; some compounds

The animals in *Badger's Parting Gifts* were **unhappy** because they missed Badger.

Unhappy is the opposite of happy.
The animals were **not** happy.

A Write out the sentences below. Change the words in **bold** to a word that is opposite. The first one has been done to help you.

1. The story was **untrue**
                        The story was **true**.
2. Dad told me to **unlock** the door.
3. I **dislike** beans.
4. Mum asked me to **unpack** my suitcase.
5. The advice my gran gave me was **unhelpful**.
6. I **disagree** with my brother.

B Mrs Rabbit can bake **gingerbread**. The word **gingerbread** is made up of two smaller words, **ginger** and **bread**.

Read the words below.
Write out the two words that have been used to make each word.

1. teapot
2. handbag
3. teaspoon
4. suitcase
5. postman

Can you think of any more words like these?

Your poster

Design a poster about Badger.

Draw a picture of him.

What was he like?

What things could he do?

What did the animals like best about him?

The Pudding Like a Night on the Sea

The pudding looked softer and lighter than air.

"Perfect!" my father said. "Now I'm going to take a nap. If something important happens, bother me. If nothing important happens, don't bother me. And – the pudding is for your mother. Leave the pudding alone!"

Huey and I guarded the pudding.

"Oh, it's a wonderful pudding," Huey said. "I wonder how it tastes."

"Leave the pudding alone," I said.

"If I just put my finger in – there – I'll know how it tastes," Huey said. And he did it.

"You did it!" I said. "How does it taste?"

"It tastes like a whole raft of lemons," he said.

"You've made a hole in the pudding! I said. "But since you did it, I'll have a taste." It tasted like floating at sea.

"That was a bigger lick than I took!" Huey said. "You put in your whole hand! Look at the pudding!"

It looked like craters on the moon.

from **The Pudding Like a Night on the Sea**
by Ann Cameron

Day 1 The pudding

A
1. Who said, "Leave the pudding alone"?
2. Who was first to try the pudding?

B
What do you think Dad will say to the boys?

Days 2 and 3 It's wonderful!

It's a wonderful pudding!

Wonderful means **full of wonder**.

Words that end in **ful** are usually describing words.

A Add **ful** to each of the words below.

1. care_ _ _
2. forget_ _ _
3. pain_ _ _
4. thought_ _ _
5. use_ _ _

B Write two or three sentences of your own using any of the words above.

Days 4 and 5 A different story

Write another story of your own about the two boys planning a surprise for their father.

What will the surprise be?

What will their father think of the surprise?

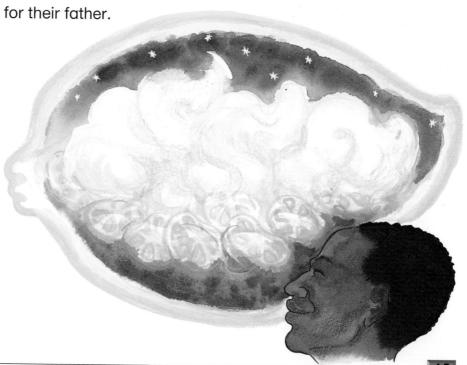

The Worst Witch

The kitten gazed at her sadly and licked her nose with its rough tongue. "Oh come on," said Mildred, softening her voice. "I'm not really angry with you. Let's try again."

And she put the kitten back on the broomstick, from which it fell with a thud. An idea flashed into Mildred's head, and she dived into the school, leaving her kitten chasing a leaf along the ground and the broomstick still patiently hovering.

She came out carrying her satchel which she hooked over the end of the broom and then bundled the kitten into it. The kitten's astounded face peeped out of the bag as Mildred flew delightedly round the yard.

from **The Worst Witch** *by Jill Murphy*

It had taken Mildred several weeks of falling off and crashing before she could ride the broomstick reasonably well, and it looked as though her kitten was going to have the same trouble. When she put it on the end of the stick, it just fell off without even trying to hold on. After many attempts, Mildred picked up her kitten and gave it a shake.

"Listen!" she said severely. "You don't even *try* to hold on. Everyone else is all right – look at all your friends."

Mildred and her kitten

A

1. What happened when Mildred put her kitten on the broomstick?
2. What was the kitten chasing along the ground?
3. What did Mildred fetch from the school?

B

1. Explain how Mildred got her kitten to stay on the broomstick.
2. What do you think Mildred's teacher will think of her idea?

Past tense

Write out the sentences below. Choose the correct word to write in each space.

A

1. When Mildred put her kitten on the broomstick, it _____ off.

   fall/fell

2. Mildred _____ out of school carrying her satchel.

   came/come

3. Mildred _____ delightedly round the yard.

   fly/flew

B

1. My cat _____ a mouse.

   catch/caught

2. I _____ Big Ben when I was in London.

   saw/see

3. We _____ to the beach last Sunday.

   go/went

Your story

Write about Mildred.

What is she like?

What would her friends say about her?

What would her teachers say about her?

Unit 23

Meet the Writers

Jill Murphy

I can't remember a time when I wasn't writing stories and drawing pictures. I was busily making little books before I even went to school.

I was actually rather a good child at primary school, where I showed such early promise, but when I went up to the grammar school at eleven, I completely changed character and became exactly like Mildred Hubble, which is why I made her the heroine of my first book *The Worst Witch*.

Writing and illustrating my own books was the only thing I ever wanted to do and I did it! You can't beat the feeling of joy which comes with that!

from **Author Profile**, *Book Trust*

Questionnaire

What was your favourite subject when you were at school? *English*

What was your worst subject? *Maths, science, games*

What is your favourite food? *Sausages, chips, beans*

Favourite own book/character: *The Worst Witch and Peace At Last*

If you could travel back in time what period would you go to? *Dinosaur Age with my son Charlie so that we could see what they really looked like*

Information about Jill Murphy

A

1. What is Jill Murphy's job?
2. What was her favourite subject when she was at school?
3. What is Jill Murphy's favourite food?

B

1. Do you think Jill Murphy enjoys her job?
2. Jill Murphy illustrates her own books. What does an **illustrator** do?

Questions

A Who is your favourite author?

Think of five questions to ask him or her.

Start each sentence with one of the question words below.

| what | when | where | who | why |

Remember to end each question with a question mark.

B Try to work out what questions were asked by reading the answers given below.

Write out the questions.

1. My favourite colour is yellow.
2. I live in London.
3. I have three brothers and no sisters.

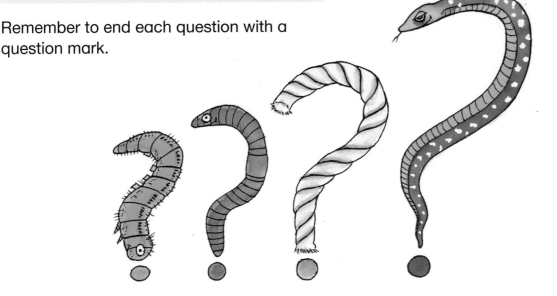

Writing about yourself

You are a writer. One day, you might write books which are sold in shops and read by many people.

Write about yourself. What is the title of the best story you have ever written? What are your likes and dislikes?

49

The Hodgeheg

"Your Auntie Betty has copped it," said Pa Hedgehog to Ma.

"Oh, no!" cried Ma. "Where?"

"Just down the road. Opposite the newsagent's. Bad place to cross, that."

"Everywhere's a bad place to cross nowadays," said Ma. "The traffic's dreadful." ...

Almost from the moment his eyes had opened, while his prickles were still soft and rubbery, Max had shown promise of being a bright boy.

"What are you talking about, Ma?" he said.

"Nothing," said Ma hastily.

"You wouldn't be talking about nothing," said Max, "or there wouldn't be any point in talking."

"Don't be cheeky," said Pa, "and mind your own business."

"Well I suppose it is their business really, Pa, isn't it?" said Ma. "They're bound to go exploring outside our garden before long, and we must warn them."

"You're right," said Pa, and he proceeded to give his children a long lecture about the problems of road safety for hedgehogs.

from **The Hodgeheg** *by Dick King-Smith*

Poor Auntie Betty!

A

1. What has happened to Auntie Betty?
2. Where did the accident happen?
3. What does Ma want to warn her children about?

B

What rules should you follow to stay safe when crossing a road?

The *ea* sound (as in head)

The traffic's dr**ea**dful.

Listen to the **ea** sound in the word dr**ea**dful.

A Read the words below aloud (but quietly) to yourself and listen to the **ea** sound. Write out the sentences, putting the correct word in each space.

bread	breakfast	feather	spread
	ready	heavy	

1. I like cornflakes for _____.
2. Dad likes white _____ but Mum prefers brown.
3. I like to _____ lots of peanut butter on my toast.
4. My brother takes ages getting _____ for school.
5. This box is very _____ but that one is as light as a _____.

B Write the missing word from each space.

1. Ready, _____, go!
2. Someone who cannot hear is _____.
3. I hope we have sunny _____ on holiday.

A safety poster

Design a poster explaining how to cross a road safely.

Football Crazy

The Nation's Favourite Game

Football, or soccer as it is sometimes called, is one of the most popular sports in Britain. A professional football team is made up of eleven players. Games usually last for ninety minutes. The team that scores the most goals wins the game.

What makes a good football player?

Football players have to be very fit. They need strong muscles and a lot of energy. Players have to follow the rules of the game and concentrate hard. It is important to be able to play well as part of a team. Even the best strikers would be unable to score goals without the support of their team mates.

Footballers wear a special kit. Each team has its own football strip – a shirt, shorts and socks. Football boots have studs on the soles which stop players from slipping.

The game

A

1. How many players are there in a football team?
2. How long does a game of football last?
3. How are football boots different from other boots?

B

What makes a good football player?

S, W

Days 2 and 3

The Contents page

This is the **Contents** page from a book about sport.

Contents	
football	2
netball	6
basketball	10
rugby	12
hockey	14
cricket	16
athletics	18
sporting awards	20
keeping fit	22

A

1. Which page would you turn to if you wanted to find out about netball?
2. Where would you look to learn about hockey?
3. What information would you find if you turned to page 16?
4. Where would you look for information about football?

B

1. Where would you look for information about exercise?
2. Where might you find out about the Olympics?
3. What information do you think might be on page 13?

T

Days 4 and 5

A writing activity

Choose one of the headings from the contents page to write about.

Use real information books to help you.

Fangs

Tap! Tap! Tap! Someone was tapping on the shop window. With a sigh, I turned around.

It was a boy. He had the most serious face I'd ever seen. The boy looked at me. I looked at him. He tapped again very gently on the shop window with his fingernail and smiled – a genuine, friendly, admiring smile. And that's when I knew! This boy was all right! I beamed back at him, giving him my biggest, cheesiest, fangiest grin.

Come into the shop, I thought. *Please* come in and buy me.

I didn't want to build up my hopes. Lost of people – men and women, boys and girls – had tapped on the window and waved. Some even smiled. But none of them ever came into the shop to buy me.

I wanted to live somewhere else. Living in a tank in the pet shop was boring. And, worse than that, it was lonely. I had a long-distant memory of the sun and the sky in another place with hundreds of my family all around me. But now it was just me.

The boy watching me mouthed, *"Wait there!"* He practically ran into the shop. Obviously my biggest, cheesiest, fangiest smile had worked!

from Fangs
by Malorie Blackman

Day 1 · T

The spider in the shop

A
1. Who was tapping on the shop window?
2. What sort of shop was it?

B
1. What did the spider think about living in the shop?
2. What do you think the boy is going to do?

S, W

Days 2 and 3

The right word

Write out the sentences below. Choose the correct word to write in each space.

Look back at the story for help.

tapped	wanted	turned	smiled

A
1. When the spider _____ around he saw a boy.
2. The boy _____ on the window and _____ at the spider.
3. The spider _____ to live somewhere else.

B Find a word in the story that means the same as the words below:

1. beamed
2. knocked
3. grin

Days 4 and 5 · T

You are the spider!

Imagine you are the spider. Write about what happens when the boy takes you to his house.

What will his mum have to say?

Will you like your new home?

Unit 27

Playing With Words

Hatch Me a Riddle

In a little white room
all round and smooth
sits a yellow moon.

In a little white room
once open, for ever open,
sits a yellow moon.

In a little white room,
with neither window nor door,
sits a yellow moon.

Who will break the walls
of the little white room
to steal the yellow moon?

A wise one or a fool?

John Agard

Hold it steady in your hand,
Then you will see another land,
Where right is left, and left is right,
And no sound stirs by day or night;
When you look in, yourself you see,
Yet in that place you cannot be.

John Cunliffe

Something I tell,
With never a word;
I keep it well,
Though it flies like a bird.

John Cunliffe

Guessing riddles

A

1. Read the first riddle. What is it about?
2. What is the **yellow moon**?
3. Can you find a clue to the riddle in the title?

B

1. Read the second riddle. What is it about?
2. The third riddle describes a clock. What is the **something** it tells?
3. Which of the three riddles do you think is best? Why?

Jokes

A Mirror Messages

Read the jokes below. Can you work out the answers?

Look at the back-to-front answers in a mirror to see if you were right.

1. What is black and white and read all over?
(A newspaper)

2. What do you call a frozen bicycle?
(An icicle)

3. What's the world's biggest mouse?
(A hippopotamus)

B Match each of the jokes below to the correct answer.

1. Where do frogs hang up their coats?

A dentist

2. What's black, white and red?

Mittens

3. What do you call someone who looks down in the mouth?

In a croak room

4. What do you get if you cross a cat with a ball of wool?

A sun-tanned zebra

Invent your own riddles

Invent some riddles of your own by describing the things in the box opposite.

Your riddles can be questions or poems.

glasses   **aeroplane**   **chair**

Bothersome Brothers

Brother

I had a little brother
And I brought him to my mother
And I said I want another
Little brother for a change.
But she said don't be a bother
So I took him to my father
And I said this little bother
Of a brother's very strange.

But he said one little brother
Is exactly like another
And every little brother
Misbehaves a bit he said.
So I took the little bother
From my mother and my father
And I put the little bother
Of a brother back to bed.

Mary Ann Hoberman

T

Getting rid of brother

A

1. Why did the girl take her little brother to her mother?
2. What did her mother reply?
3. What did the girl's father tell her?
4. What did the girl do in the end?

B

Write down all the different words you can find that end in **er**.

Words that mean the same

How many times is the word **little** used in the poem?

> The poet has repeated words in an interesting way. But it is best not to repeat the same words too many times when writing stories. You can use other words that mean the same.

A

Write another word that means the same as each of the words below.

| sad | small | large | cook | yell |

1. tiny
2. big
3. unhappy

4. shout
5. bake

B

Write out the following sentences. Change each word in **bold** to another word that means the same.

There was once a **tiny** old woman who lived in a **nice** little cottage beside a stream. When it was sunny she **liked** walking in the woods. If the weather was **nasty** she would sit next to the fire and knit **lovely** things for her grandchildren.

A funny poem

Write a funny poem about an imaginary member of your family. Try to think of a word to describe them that begins with the same letter. Here are some ideas:

a bother of a brother
a sensible sister
a daring dad
a merry mum
a grumpy grandad

Communication

How Do We Communicate?

When we communicate, we pass on information, ideas or feelings to others. We communicate in many different ways, by using words, sounds, movement and pictures. We can communicate without even saying a word. A smile can mean, "I like you", a frown can mean, "I feel worried."

We often use machines to communicate.

The radio brings words and music into our homes. Radios pick up sound waves sent from a radio station.

The television brings sounds and pictures from around the world into our homes.

We can talk to people all over the world on the telephone.

A fax machine copies writing and pictures, and sends them to a fax machine in another town or country.

Computers are the most powerful form of communication. Messages and pictures can be sent rapidly from one computer to another, thousands of kilometres away by e-mail. The Internet is like a gigantic encyclopedia.

Ways to communicate

A

1. Name some of the ways we communicate.
2. Name one machine that brings words and music into our homes.
3. Name a machine that lets us talk to people far away.

B

Name as many uses of the computer as you can think of.

Fact and fiction

A

Read and copy the sentences below. Write **fact** or **fiction** after each sentence.

1. Radios bring words and music into our homes.
2. The princess kissed a frog and he turned into a handsome prince.
3. The Ice Dragon carried Lao Lao on his back.
4. We can use computers to send e-mail.

A fact is something which we know to be true. Fiction is something which has been made up.

B

1. Write a sentence of your own that is **fact**.
2. Write a sentence that is **fiction**.

Your information book

Make an information book of your own about machines we use in our homes. Think about the ways in which they help us. Begin by thinking about the machines in your kitchen. Use writing and pictures to make your book as interesting as possible.

A caption is a short description that goes with a picture.

Write captions to go with your pictures.

Little Red Riding Hood and the Wolf

As soon as Wolf began to feel
That he would like a decent meal,
He went and knocked on Grandma's door.
When Grandma opened it, she saw
The sharp white teeth, the horrid grin,
And Wolfie said, "May I come in?"
Poor Grandmamma was terrified,
"He's going to eat me up!" she cried.
And she was absolutely right.
He ate her up in one big bite.
But Grandmamma was small and tough,
And Wolfie wailed, "That's not enough!
I haven't yet begun to feel
That I have had a decent meal!"
He ran around the kitchen yelping,
"I've *got* to have another helping!"
Then added with a frightful leer,
"I'm therefore going to wait right here
Till Little Miss Red Riding Hood
Comes home from walking in the wood."

from **Revolting Rhymes**
by ***Roald Dahl***

A hungry wolf

A

1. Which famous story is this rhyme about?
2. Who did the wolf eat?
3. Who does he want to eat next?

B

1. Who wrote this rhyme?
2. Can you think of another story or rhyme by the same writer?

Rhyming pairs

A Write out the words from the poem in rhyming pairs. Do it like this pair: **leer, here**

feel	bite	hood	meal
grin	in	right	wood

B Draw a picture of the wolf and write a few sentences about him. Don't forget his sharp white teeth and horrid grin!

The rest of the story

Can you remember the story of Little Red Riding Hood? What happens next? Write out the rest of the story in your own words.